The Devil's Tattoo

Brett Evans

indigo dreams poetry
Indigo Dreams Publishing

First Edition: The Devil's Tattoo
First published in Great Britain in 2015 by:
Indigo Dreams Publishing Ltd
24 Forest Houses
Halwill
Beaworthy
EX21 5UU
www.indigodreams.co.uk

ISBN 978-1-909357-78-5

British Library Cataloguing in Publication Data. A CIP record for this book can be obtained from the British Library.

Designed and typeset in Palatino Linotype by Indigo Dreams.
Cover design Ronnie Goodyer at Indigo Dreams.
Printed and bound in Great Britain by 4edge Ltd.
www.4edge.co.uk

Papers used by Indigo Dreams are recyclable products made from wood grown in sustainable forests following the guidance of the Forest Stewardship Council.

CONTENTS

Acknowledgements are due to the editors of the following magazines and ezines where some of these poems (or earlier incarnations of them) first appeared:

Black Light Engine Room, Butcher's Dog, Clear Poetry, The English Chicago Review, The Frogmore Papers, Ink, Sweat & Tears, The Interpreter's House, The Journal, Other Poetry, Snakeskin.

'Directed by Sergio Leone' (p26) was a runner up in the 2012 Cardiff International Poetry Competition and first appeared on the Literature Wales website.

I would like to thank my very dear friends Wendy Pratt and Phil Robertson who endured the relentless torture of going over draft after draft of these poems – that's friendship indeed. Without them *The Devil's Tattoo* would not have been possible. So now you know just who to lynch, tar and feather.

Thanks are also due to Judi Sutherland for her attention, input and feedback over the years.

The Devil's Tattoo

Marshes

Before the seasons threatened girls
we swashbuckled summers across the weir,
busied winters skating fields;
our ugly, lovely children's world.

We chased the heron to skies as grey
as age; his glorious, idle hours
spent sentry over marshes, rivers,
annexed by eager boys at play.

Heat and squall saw our invasions,
the souvenir of blue-black mud -
trickle, smudge, or cake or clod -
proud war paint of initiation.

No spirits drew us to the marshes,
nor had our dormant Celtic blood
ever been spilt on countless blades
of grass from here to Rhuddlan Castle;

imprinted on that Godless ground,
in hidden dips and boggy ditches
settled by water rats and leeches,
was Edward's unforgiving crown.

Taids[1] would tell of Llywelyn's men
as 'sleeping dragons who woke at dusk',
believing those Welsh dead had thirst
to die by Edward once again;

---

[1] Welsh, Grandfathers

that when the sun had sunk to Hell,
then Edward's dead, Llywelyn's dead,
would rise up from the mires, they said,
their swords blood-rusted to the hilt.

Us boys, we braved it out one night,
clamped between stone bridge and stars.
Unseeing eyes caused untuned ears
to hear wind, reed, and river fight;

the splashing dash of water rat
became the clash of steel on steel,
the owl's wing beat, mace on shield.
Yet running home I once looked back

and never had it seemed so calm.
Dear Taid, your taids could not restore
Wales with tales of ancient wars.
Diolch yn fawr,[2] *we're who we are.*

---

[2] Welsh, thank you very much

Portrait of the Piss Artist as a Young Boy

I was pissed, of course, but they tell me this is how it was:
I staggered down their drive, not mine, warbling,
I'm off to join the IRA and I'm off tomorrow morn
my keys scratching at their door, they opened it,
And we're all off to Dublin in the green, in the green
I lunged through the kitchen,
Where the helmets glisten in the sun
stumbled to the living room,
Where the bayonets flash and the rifles crash
and slumped comfortably onto the sofa.
To the rattle of a Thompson gun.
I was more surprised than them to realise
I was in the wrong fecking house,
Bejaysus, don't tell Hannah.
But I do remember you boys, God love you.
You'd been allowed to stay up late.
And I remember you, the youngest,
white-blond you were back then.
Green eyes wide and round as your mouth;
no shock, just some mischievous epiphany.
A decade later it's you singing your way home,
unsteady, though at the right door.
It's been one helluva session, but I fear time
being called and that I won't be stopping for much longer now.
Before I go I want to know what you saw that night.
Surely no hero or secon' Da, not me.
Was it just the prospect, at that young age,
of a grown man hell-bent on having fun?

In Bed with Ma Rainey

I dreamt I was in bed with Ma Rainey -
both of us being fat and ugly, glutted
from hedonism, we seemed the perfect pair.
She encouraged me to plough deep
into the Mother of the Blues; ply her
with southern comfort, pig out on jelly roll.
After I'd made her moan, she took me
to her breast and sang; *Jelly Bean Blues*
trembled up through her glorious chest
and she knew she was the most beautiful of ugly things.
Midas would have traded everything to be her;
I swear it was her voice that turned her teeth to gold.

Scarecrow

Reaping nothing from what's been sown,
arms outstretched, forsaken,
he wears his unkempt crown; king
of the hand-me-down. Dressed
forever in the same tattered rags

that suck the wind through or hang
from his frame with the weight
of the morning's rain, he sways;
a metronome to an orchestra
of gale and sleet. This son of Man

is blind to purpose, rooted in solitude
and cannot find a voice to yawp
back into the squall; no sermons,
no parables, no disciples or flock.
Not even the birds.

Poem for Larry McMurtry

My Peckinpah of the page, it seems our heroes
have always been cowboys. And whenever Ramblin' Jack sang
I'm sure we rode with him on the trail of the buffalo.
Yet the crew I hooked up with knew nothing of Mustangs,
could sing lonesome songs but broke no broncos,
and their faces, though aged by weather, were reddened, not tanned.
They never chewed tobacco while riding the Llano;
the furthest they dared to move when smoking was banned
was to slide their arses off barstools and head out westwards
(the young and the old, the able, the fat and the thin)
to be silhouetted in doorways like Ethan Edwards.
Your Texas towns and this Welsh one could be twinned.
If I rode west, would adventures wait for me
in Colwyn Bay, Bangor, Holyhead, Dun Laoghaire?

Notes from Colwyn Bay

Cooling the obsidian sweat of the tarmac,
and blistering red-brick terrace
of Llewellyn Road,
a lone saxophone blows
notes as blue as the bay;
a Welsh mistral.

This Coltrane-kissed breeze gently rattles
the redundant armoured shutters
of empty shops, and the flush-faced
cattle anxious for slaughter
come opening time.

Net curtains in half-closed windows keep
rhythm, slow and sensuous, relieved
to hear some melody
other than a maverick bus,
the unoiled Job Centre's door,
the taxi rank's white noise,
and Danny-bloody-Boy come midnight.
A lament for, and from, the anonymous.

The coda is played by neighbours and bailiffs
too deaf to hear that his blues
are theirs, and a eulogy
for the whole miserable-bastard town.

Teaching Jesus to Dance

It's hard, you said, when the Devil's on your back;
you climb up *his* gnarled sequoia spine
vertebrae by vertebrae, your glass
steady; do not spill a drop. Lupine
being the order of this and every night,
sink your teeth into that toughest cut
of meat: the neck. He'll writhe, so grasp your pint,
employ your weight till the bastard breaks; enough
of this should see his hooves are shorn, have bled.
Once his tail's been dragged out the dance hall door,
it's time we tucked the moon into its bed
and howl in another unexpected dawn.
And let's not dwell upon the Devil's faults,
tonight we've a date with him for another waltz.

Stepping Out for a Cigarette

I leave them at the bar laughing
after some quip at their expense - their plaudits
fade as I step out for a smoke.

Sparking up, I am elongated by the sensor light.
Christ, it almost makes me thin. There, I'm projected
over untrue tarmac; heel of downpipe and drain;

midriff to head staggering up the fire escape;
every motion of hand to mouth detected
by the Orwellian bulb. The revellers inside

would be unnerved to see me looming,
so dark - like a shadow on the lung.

Song for Swinging Drunkards

My affinity
is with the rain;
it pours, falls, calms
then pours again.

Portrait of Dylan Thomas, oil on canvas by Augustus John

It's not so strange, the opinion that a poet needs to be slapped,
but the desire to kiss you, Thomas, winded me like a shovel-hook.
Those two red, too red lips that had mothered vowels and spat
consonants; those 'hold that pose while the artist fucks
your wife-to-be' eyes, of course, betray no surprise.
Through callousness or genius, John laid down his brushes
and denied you tears – yet captured
that trinity: beast, angel and madman; Dylan.

And so it is those lips I wish to kiss to stop you cursing,
that face I'd slap to turn those brimming eyes away.
Still, now's far too late to curl a finger through one red ringlet,
pull you to my chest and whisper There, there, boy.
Lovers don't matter anymore than artists. Or poets.

Anticipating Pints of Stout

The snow settles on my shoulders;
this long, dark coat hugging my corpulent carcass
as I wait beneath the swinging sign of The Magpie.
I consider the pints, part drawn, lined up along the bar,
awaiting their complementary rolling thunder.
It's a shiver not a shake that you witness -
note the weather, temperature.
Soon she'll lift the latch and call the faithful.
With salvation on tap, the light of the world will be brighter
the more of the black stuff I pour into myself; a lechery
of pint-sized priests to knock back without repentance.
And the barmaid with the palest skin
and darkest grin who is all too accustomed
to the contrasts between night and day
will play my film noir femme fatale 'til closing time.
Too soon I'll stagger out on to beguiling snow,
not giving two fucks about black ice below.

Triolet to a Barmaid

I swear to God there'll be another one,
there always is. You come and bloody go
and kid the drunk his love's so fucking strong
he'll swear to God there'll be no other one
that he would serve; to pamper with oils and run
her bath and lather her hair to a Guinness foam.
I swear to God there'll be another one,
there always is; you come and bloody go.

Not Raglan Road

The spit, piss and vomit of Bridge Street;
Market Street's chewing-gum tattoos and flaking
dog-end scabs have all too often kissed the soles
of her suede boots. The leaves and litter sent flailing
over the kerb by motorists are bruised beneath
their tread. On a day like this, a handful
of raindrops may just find their resting place
in her hair. And as she passes the Pen-y-Bont,
the water of the Gele is pulled over troublesome stones
toward her. Past The Gwindy now,
and from the shops the fragrances of coffee
and pastries whisper perfume-like
about her naked wrists and throat. I watch
as I sit in this third pub from the sun
and she arrives at the crossing.
There is only her moving through this world;
the cars have stopped, the traffic lights
embarrassed for me.

Carving a Lovespoon

I'm taking my axe to the trunk of the living tree;
much more convincing than my awkward tongue
would be a poem carved from the greenwood

of the sycamore. Once that's felled, I'll split a stretch of bole
in one concentrated strike, then saw a block
from this half-mooned stem on which to draw the spoon.

Long evenings dedicated to carving with my pocket knife
as if each shave would find me further underneath your skin.
Such work is slow, attentive; a fantasized unclothing -

imagination journeying ahead of hands.
I'll have shaped at the base a deep and generous bowl;
above, a dragon for your protection

and a decorative stem leading up to an off centre
heart. Yet, even timber is tongue-tied so this symbol
shall never feel heat from your palms; it will instead hang,

a mocking effigy. And the Celtic knot in my stomach
will inspire the blade once more, for I'll score that hard heart,
witness seasons of dust settle into the scar.

Stepping Stone

It's something you weekenders
would never know. You who only dip your toe
on a Friday night, who only paddle
the shallows on match day, or maybe
even ford the stream
on a bank holiday afternoon.

You have never hurled yourself to rent
the sheen of water, sink
and remain flat on your back
on the river bed
until you cease to feel
the chill or see your skin
begin to wrinkle.
Let me tell you how it is.

Just place your foot on that first
unstable stepping stone,
and mid-step, challenge your own balance
in anticipation of a slip into the drink.
Arms outstretched,
you're not quite walking
on water, not yet steeped
in faith but fighting
the temptation of turbulence.

Once both feet are on the stone,
before taking another step,
look down. Look long and hard
at your reflection on the water,
then deeper to name
the fish that ripples through your core,
to spy what lies
half-buried in the shale.

And through all this, clenched in the fist
like a fretting butterfly, the desire
to be dry.

Positions in Bed

My right cheekbone rests on a crucifix
of forearms, one calf tucked
across the back of a knee; some unconscious
attempt at achieving symmetry.

Lying on my left, only legs
beneath the covers, one arm
thrown over to hold her, forehead
pressed to the neck of an imagined lover.

Not quite corner to corner, shoulder
and head loll off the edge, one ankle
roughly kisses the other; staggering
between dream pubs the whole wild night.

And sat upright, the whole dry day
ahead to think on wild nights,
dreams once savoured, loves
imagined, and if crucifixion

did not mean vocation;
some days on the cross, some off.

Reading Sean O'Brien in the Bath

On the first floor of an ex-council house
this fat, pink alchie reads O'Brien in the bath.
At his shoulder the pint glass of cider mocks

his sweating face. The cold tap drips - he lifts
his eyes from the book - for how long
it's dripped he's not clear. Each drop

a year: he counts through teens and twenties,
stops at mid-thirties, leans forward, halts the drops
with a twist of his hand. *I could write a poem,* he thinks,

if I could turn my life around, break habits, routines, totter
forward, baby-like and lift a title to work from.
He's kidding himself of course; a day off the sauce

is a year on a chain gang - the hammer
chipping away. His reverie is smashed
as our hero wakes to the fact

that something is amiss; had he hauled his bulk
out from the tub just to take a piss?

Directed by Sergio Leone

There's nothing but waiting around to die, so you choose
how to spend that time: swatting flies on your stubbled
throat whilst waiting for a train or riding through
this one-horse world, hell-bent on creed or trouble.
A bottle of rye, a cheroot beneath the bough
may be enough for those who're simply chasing
a quieter life. Or you could stand or slouch
between hero, villain, gunslinger and assassin;
your idle fingers twitching whilst waiting on a script
to reveal the character to which you are assigned.
An extra in another's movie, too late you've grasped
that at the bar, in bed, on the street, dying's just dying.
Your final suspicion, that there must have been so much more;
that there must have been music, an unforgettable score.

Like Louis Armstrong Practically Rewrote Stardust

I'm grabbing the standard by the balls;
the familiar must become unfamiliar.
No wondering why I've spent the lonely nights
dreaming of a song: too many days conducted
beating the Devil's tattoo on the bars. I'm taking
control of this tune now. I've the choice where to take
the melody, and break lyrics everyone thought writ.

Orchestra members step back, I'm bringing myself
to the fore. Shaky hands will grasp resolve
between sweaty palms, morning-after lips
balmed with anticipation.

Kings, Castles, Rascals

This stone bridge was once a castle.
From here we rained down missiles;
or as jeering warriors stormed
full pelt up the grass bank, our flailing
branches ready to knock the crowns
right off each others' cocky blocks.

How long ago your fighting spirits died.
No laughter or battle cries from you today:
just the cosy life far away from campaigns raged
across schoolyards, fields, then towns and pubs. Dutifully
glued to whatever trite shite is watched by wife
or sprog, you lie on fat sofas - the glorious dead.

Now the parapet barely reaches my knees
and the river a much less formidable moat
than I'd have sworn; though the Gele's tears
still pour over the weir, sad to lose identity
in the vast, salt Irish Sea. And me?
I haunt our stomping grounds, my shadow striding
out before me: a giant ghost, coat flapping in the wind.
And the water before the weir forever lapping at the child.

Indigo Dreams Publishing
24 Forest Houses
Halwill
Beaworthy
Devon
EX21 5UU
United Kingdom